DEPARTMENT OF THE ENVIRONMENT

AUDLEY END

ESSEX

LONDON
HER MAJESTY'S STATIONERY OFFICE
1958

E. AUD. 728.83

ISBN 0 11 670124 2

AUDLEY END

HISTORY

AUDLEY END is one of the most famous of the many stately mansions which have been the glory of the English countryside for the past four hundred years. Like their medieval predecessors, the castles, they are or were the centres of large estates with a complicated organisation of tenants and servants revolving round them. But, whereas castles were built when the owner had often to keep in mind the danger of armed attack, in the mansion the noble lord or other owner could give his undivided attention to the arts of peace. It is indeed to these lords that the country owes, not only many a fine house, but also much which is now admired in wood and field. For it should always be remembered that in its present form the English countryside is not a work of nature, but a product of the hand of man. That man, more often than not, was the local squire.

This house is not as old as the name it bears. The latter commemorates Sir Thomas Audley, from 1529 to 1535 Speaker of the Parliament which passed the Acts for the Suppression of the Monasteries. Amongst the gifts with which King Henry VIII rewarded him for this and other services was the abbey of Walden, which stood on the site of the house and its immediate surroundings, *i.e.* towards the western end of the town of Saffron Walden. While there are no upstanding parts of the Benedictine abbey of Walden, remains of the monastic buildings still surviving beneath the floors of the house suggest that the inner court lying behind the hall marks the site of the cloister. Likewise nothing

Thomas, first Lord Audley (1488–1544), who acquired the monastery of Walden on the site of which the house is built

recognisable remains from the first Audley End built by Sir Thomas Audley. This Sir Thomas later was created Lord Audley of Walden and remained in royal favour until his death in 1544. His tomb, a noteworthy one in black marble, may be seen in Saffron Walden church. Lord Audley's property, including the land on which the later house was built, in due course descended to Thomas Howard, son of the fourth Duke of Norfolk, who was beheaded on Tower Hill in 1572. Tom Howard commanded a ship in the fleet which defeated the Spanish Armada in 1588, and was knighted for his gallantry in the action. As he continued to distinguish himself at sea, Queen Elizabeth I made him Baron Howard of Walden in 1597 and a Knight of the Garter the following year.

His father had been beheaded for intriguing with Mary, Queen of Scots. It is therefore not surprising that when in 1603 Mary's son James ascended the English throne as James I, he set himself to make atonement to the family of the dead duke. Lord Howard was created Earl of Suffolk and made Lord Chamberlain, and in 1614 became Lord High Treasurer of England. In 1605, as Lord Chamberlain, he was largely responsible for the discovery in the vaults of the House of Peers of the combustibles prepared for the Gunpowder Plot.

The declining years of the earl were marred by charges of embezzle-

Margaret (died 1563), Lord Audley's daughter, who married the fourth Duke of Norfolk and so brought the house to the Howard family

ment. In 1618 he was deprived of his office, committed to the Tower of London, and after trial fined £30,000. Public opinion at the time attributed his fall to the activities of Catherine Knevit, a celebrated beauty, whom he married after the death of his first wife. It seems to have been notorious that she extorted money from those who had business at the Treasury in return for using her influence with her husband in their favour. He, in turn, was excessively indulgent to his family, who repaid him by causing his disgrace.

It was the Earl of Suffolk who built the great Audley End. All records of its erection have been lost; indeed it has been stated that they were deliberately destroyed. It is supposed to have been begun in 1603, the year of James I's accession, and to have taken thirteen years to build. Similarly the cost must remain a matter of conjecture, although it was rumoured that Suffolk told the King that the whole building, with its furniture, cost £200,000—a fantastic sum by early 17th-century standards. Small wonder that King James is said to have remarked that the house was too large for a King, though it might do for a Lord Treasurer. In view of the circumstances of the earl's disgrace not long afterwards, the King's remark may well have been true, even if apocryphal.

In order to appreciate the remark to the full, one must realise that

French 16th-century chair which was once in the possession of the poet Alexander Pope. This form of chair is known as caquetoire

the house, when complete, was vastly bigger than the present mansion. It completely enclosed two square courtyards. From drawings of the house made before parts were demolished, it is possible to visualise the appearance of the building in its prime.

It was approached from the west by a bridge over the river Cam and along an avenue, flanked by two rows of lime trees, to a grand entrance gateway with four circular towers. The main rooms on the north and south sides of the principal or western court were on the first floor, built over an open piazza or walk and supported on columns of alabaster. On the eastern side of this court there was a terrace of slight elevation, parallel with the present hall. Beyond the hall was the inner court, which was completely enclosed with ranges of rooms. Of this house only three sides of the inner court remain, the whole of the outer court and the eastern side of the inner court having been demolished.

The design of the house is important in the development of English architecture, for Audley End was one of the first great buildings in England to display the Anglo-Flemish style which marks the first years of the 17th century. It was the work of Bernard Johnson, who also designed Northumberland House in the Strand for Henry Howard, Earl of Northampton, uncle of the Earl of Suffolk, the builder of Audley End. Henry Howard, like his nephew whose early education he largely supervised, prospered under James I, being created Earl of Northampton by that monarch in 1604. The older man was a considerable scholar and may be regarded as a patron of architecture, and at Audley End we may well see an example of his influence both in the overall design of his nephew's house and in the choice of Johnson as architect.

Since the 17th century the house has been the subject of much demolition and subsequent restoration and even partial rebuilding. As a result there is now little to be seen of the original structure. The two porches and some of the walling of the hall date from the 17th century, as do the arches and columns on the ground floor of the south side of the south wing, but otherwise there is nothing whatever left visible of the building of the Earl of Suffolk. Internally the only works of his time still in position in the rooms open to the public are the wooden screen in the hall and the stone arcade just to the north of it, as well as the two doorways in the east wall of the hall and the ceiling and chimney-piece in the saloon. A number of Jacobean overmantels remain in the north wing, some probably moved from elsewhere in the house. Everything else, whatever its style, dates from the 18th or early 19th century. One of the noteworthy features of Audley End is that successive owners almost without exception have taken care to ensure that their own work should harmonise with the original 17th-century features. They succeeded so well that at first sight the new work may often be mistaken for the old.

The Earl of Suffolk, although disgraced, continued to live at Audley End until his death in 1626. He was succeeded by his eldest son, Theophilus, who died in 1640 after some years of ill-health. James, the eldest son of Theophilus, succeeded as the third earl. He found the estate sadly encumbered with debts, but continued to live in the house. He took little part in the Civil War between King and Parliament, and contrived to keep his property during the Commonwealth, living in privacy at Audley End. Nevertheless he remained in favour with Charles II after the Restoration in 1660.

The King indeed took a fancy to the house. The royal mansions had suffered severe damage during the Civil War and Commonwealth, and

Samuel Pepys, the diarist, who played his flageolet in the cellars of Audley End in 1677

Charles required another palace. After three or four years of negotiations Lord Suffolk sold Audley End to the King in 1669 for £50,000. By the following year the Court was established at what was then called the New Palace, and it remained in occasional use by successive sovereigns until 1701, when it was conveyed back again to its former family in the person of Henry, fifth Earl of Suffolk, in lieu of the balance of the purchase money.

There seem to be no structural features in the house to illustrate this royal occupation except a few rainwater-heads, three of the time of James II and one of the reign of William and Mary. This period is notable, however, for the fact that the Clerk of the Works, under the Surveyor General of Works, Christopher Wren, was Henry Winstanley, a man who took the trouble to record by plans and views the aspect of the Audley End of his day. Related to subsequent work at the house, Winstanley's views are invaluable. They show not only what was the appearance of the vast mansion in its prime, but also that the restorers of the 18th century faithfully copied the old features and so preserved the general appearance of a Stuart mansion.

The house had now been in existence for nearly a century. Grandiose from the beginning, after the time of its builder it had hardly ever been used to the full in a manner commensurate with its size. The maintenance of so gigantic a structure would tax the resources of any family, however wealthy. But now, in the early 18th century, the family itself began to fail. Between 1690 and 1745, when the line failed with the death, childless and intestate, of the tenth earl, there were no fewer than seven holders of the title.

In about 1721 the seventh earl consulted the architect Sir John Vanbrugh, and by his advice three sides of the great outer or western courtyard were demolished. Other buildings which housed the kitchen, chapel, etc., were also demolished at the same time or soon after, so that by the time of the last Earl of Suffolk to reside in the house all that remained was the complete inner court.

At the same time Vanbrugh made a few additions or alterations in the part of the mansion which was left standing. In place of the southern wall of the hall, which up to that time had been solid except for a doorway at the eastern end, he built a stone arcade of two tiers with three arches in each. From this arcade two flights of stairs with gilt iron balustrades were also constructed at this time, as is evident from the form of the ironwork. The plaster ceiling above Vanbrugh made in the manner of the Stuarts of the early 17th century, who delighted in wide strapwork, but he made the shape of the straps to include the same broken curve as may be seen in the balustrade, and his decoration within the strapwork is purely of 18th-century style. This is the earliest example in Audley End of the conscious copying of old motifs, which constantly recurs in the house.

In 1747, after complicated legal proceedings, the house and park were acquired by Lady Portsmouth. The building was becoming dilapidated and its total demolition was at one time under consideration. Lady Portsmouth, in her desire to adapt the house for the use of her nephew and successor, finally listened to the advice of a firm of London builders, and ordered the demolition of the eastern range of buildings. This was in or shortly after 1749. But it was soon found that this was a mistaken policy. The eastern range had contained a long gallery, not only a very

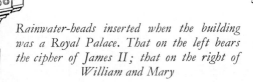

Rainwater-heads inserted when the building was a Royal Palace. That on the left bears the cipher of James II; that on the right of William and Mary

The first Lord Braybrooke, (1719–97), for whom Robert Adam redecorated the ground floor of the south wing. It was he who created the present Chapel and in 1785 reconstructed the Saloon

fine room, but also a means of communication between the north and south ranges of buildings. With the gallery no longer in existence, another means of access was needed. By 1762, when Lady Portsmouth died, an open arcade had been built beside the east wall of the hall to provide this access, and the broken eastern ends of the north and south wings had been finished off by means of single-storey buildings, ending in bay windows.

Lady Portsmouth bequeathed all her possessions to her nephew, Sir John Griffin Whitwell, on condition that he changed his name to Sir John Griffin Griffin. This he did. He had a distinguished military career, eventually becoming a field marshal. In 1784 he succeeded to the barony of Howard de Walden, and in 1788 was created Baron Braybrooke. He died in 1797 at Audley End.

Lord Braybrooke, or Lord Howard as he was usually called, was the creator of Audley End as it is seen today. He is said to have spent £100,000 on the building in days when such a figure was worth far more than it is now. Immediately after inheriting the property he rebuilt the gallery beside the east wall of the hall, adding the first-floor passage above it; this was done by 1765. He may also have repaired the stonework of the western side of the hall, because there is a rainwater-head dated 1766 beside the north porch. At about the same time he had the living suite on the ground floor of the south wing redecorated by

The south end of the Hall

Towards the north end of the Hall, showing the screen of 1605

The Chapel reconstructed in 1786 in gothic style

The Main Library

Robert Adam. Besides the rooms still visible this suite included a library in the bay at the end of the wing, but the decoration no longer exists and the room was subdivided when the books were transferred to the new library on the first floor.

Work on the house and in the grounds continued for over twenty years. Much of the external stonework was replaced with new, including all the window jambs, sills, lintels and mullions. In these, as also in the balustrades at the top of the walls, great pains were taken to imitate the old work in form, if not always in exact detail. Careful scrutiny will show minute differences, but the general effect is the same as that given by the old work. That is why Audley End still gives the appearance of being an early 17th-century mansion, although in fact almost every part of it now visible dates from the late 18th century or later.

The apartment known as the saloon was at this time quite transformed in character. The date 1785 appears above the main door in the north end, and in the northernmost panel of the west wall there is an inscription recording the fact that by this year the room was refitted. It implies that the ceiling was in no way affected. The other decoration is composed of copies of various types of ornament to be found in earlier work in the house, but it is differently executed and could not be confused with genuine work of the 17th century. Moreover the clusters of three columns beside each of the painted panels are unmistakable examples of late 18th-century or 'Strawberry Hill' Gothic, a style in use for the whole of the chapel, which was complete by November 1786. But the work on both the saloon and the chapel had been in progress for some time, and there is evidence for Robert Adam having been concerned at least in the preliminary design for these rooms.

Other work was done at the same time, such as the embellishment of the bedrooms on the first floor of the south wing, and the completion of the bay windows at the eastern ends of the two wings, as they now exist.

As the first Lord Braybrooke had no children, on his death in 1797 his property and title passed to Richard Aldworth Neville, his kinsman. In 1825 he was succeeded by his son, Richard Neville, the third Lord Braybrooke. These two possessors of Audley End were responsible for the final embellishment of the house. Begun at the end of the life of the second Lord Braybrooke, and continued by his son, the work involved the complete interchange of ground-floor and first-floor apartments in the south wing. Instead of a dining room, drawing rooms, and library on the ground floor with saloon and bedrooms on the first floor, there were now dining room, drawing room, and libraries beside the saloon on the first floor with bedrooms below. The reason for this change is

A painting by Canaletto showing the Campanile and the Doge's Palace in Venice with the Bucintoro moored alongside

not stated by the third Lord Braybrooke, who completed it and wrote a most informative and discriminating book on the house, but it may have been carried out in order that all the principal rooms should range with the saloon on one floor. The rooms on the first floor are also, of course, much loftier and have a better prospect than those below.

The present library was fitted between 1820 and 1825, as is indicated by plans still in the house, and similarity of treatment in the ceilings shows that the dining room, drawing room, and south library belong to the same scheme. Some of the plaster work in the eastern part of the dining room may be of somewhat earlier date, and the chimney-piece in the library is a genuine early 17th-century work, taken from the

14

The third Lord Braybrooke (1783–1858), to whom is due the present arrangement of the house, in particular the Main Library

north wing. But it has white and gold paint and coloured embellishments which date from 1825 or later. On the other hand the chimney-pieces in the dining room are imitations of 17th-century work and must have been fitted with royal arms to commemorate the sovereigns who once possessed the house. Throughout the house there is evidence of infinite care to rebuild and embellish it in a manner in keeping with the original work, and the inscription in the saloon gives the reason, namely gratitude to those ancestors from whom the family derived its possessions.

Of later work there is little. The arcade along the east side of the hall was filled in about 1865 and the chimney-piece in the gallery above dates from about the same time. The house was the residence of the Lords Braybrooke until the death of the seventh in 1941. It is now the property of the nation and is vested in the Department of the Environment. In 1971 the bulk of the furniture and fittings, together with a proportion of the library and a limited number of pictures, were purchased for the nation out of the Land Fund. Many of the remaining items including the great majority of the paintings which remain the property of the Hon. Robin Neville, the son of the present Lord Braybrooke, have by his courtesy been left in the rooms for the continued enjoyment of visitors. He has also presented most of the historic archives of the estate to the Essex Record Office, Chelmsford, where students who desire to consult them will be welcomed.

DESCRIPTION

Although built at the time of transition from medieval to modern styles in planning, and subjected since that time to alterations, Audley End yet retains much of the appearance of a medieval house. It may be mentioned that John Evelyn, the diarist, in 1654 described it as 'a mixt fabrick, twixt antiq and modern'. So indeed it was, not only in his day, but even at the time it was built. The original ornament which survives is Renaissance in style. So were the colonnades of the outer court, long since demolished. Yet the plan of the main house was, and in part still is, purely medieval. Other houses of the early 17th century, like Holland House in London, were then being built in a new style without a great hall, but Audley End has its hall, its screen, gallery, and passage, precisely as have many houses two or three centuries earlier in date.

The existence of two entrance porches is unusual. They are both original and their decorative motifs and doors are notable examples of

A self-portrait of the artist, Sir Peter Lely, who with his friend Hugh May, architect for the alterations to Windsor Castle and a commissioner for rebuilding London after the Great Fire

their kind. The southern porch was designed to give quick access to the high table in the hall by means of a passage behind it, but the later addition of the stone stair at the southern end of the hall caused its disuse. In the east wall of the hall, however, there is still the doorway which answered to this porch, just as there is a doorway in the same wall opposite to the northern porch.

LOBBY

Visitors now assemble in a lobby immediately north of the hall. The arcade here is original, *i.e.* early 17th-century work, and the lobby is but an enlarged version of the screens passage, normal at the lower end of all medieval halls. From it there was originally a passage to the kitchen, buttery, and pantry, but the original dispositions of this part of the house cannot now be traced and the north wall of the lobby has been altered.

The lobby is sparsely furnished, but visitors should note the mahogany side-table, carved with flutes and paterae in the Adam style, which stands against the east wall. From the ceiling hang a number of leather fire buckets dated 1833 and painted with Lord Braybrooke's initial and coronet. On the east wall hangs Winstanley's engraving of *The Royal Palace of Audley End* in 1676. Henry Winstanley of Littlebury, better known as the designer of the original Eddystone Lighthouse, was Clerk of the Works at Audley End to Charles II and James II and in 1688 he published a set of twenty-four plans and views of Audley End, dedicated to James II, the Earl of Suffolk, and Sir Christopher Wren.

HALL

It is difficult now to visualise the proportions and appearance of the hall when first built because of the alterations made early in the 18th century, when the staircase was added at the southern end. The great screen at the northern end is one of the most elaborate of its kind. The freshness of the surface is due to the fact that the whole was once covered with white paint, which was later removed. The upper part has open-work carving, because there is a gallery behind it in the medieval fashion.

The panelling on the walls is of comparatively recent date. It was put up by the third Lord Braybrooke in the second quarter of the 19th century in place of the original which had decayed. In his book he speaks of the chimney-piece as if it were original work, but it contains some unusual features and may well have been made, or remade, in the

Details of the Hall screen: garlands of fruit and vegetables, and (opposite) two rusticated arches in perspective, flanked by terms

time of the seventh Earl of Suffolk (1718–22), whose arms adorn the central panel. The figures in the recesses are not part of the original design. The ceiling is of plaster divided into many panels by wooden beams supported on brackets; in the panels are crests and cognisances of the Howard family. It is uncertain how much of this ceiling is genuine work of the 17th century.

The stone screen at the southern end of the hall and the double stair-case of stone with gilt iron balustrade are attributed to Vanbrugh. If, as seems likely, the cipher below the coronet in the balustrade is that of Charles William (C.W.), seventh Earl of Suffolk, then this alteration must have been initiated, if not actually completed, before 1722. It seems, however, that the stair has been altered somewhat since Van-brugh's day. The plaster ceiling above the staircase is Jacobean in general style, but the curves of the strapwork closely resemble those of the ironwork in the balustrade. It is therefore most likely that the ceiling is also the work of Vanbrugh, working in the Jacobean manner, no doubt under instruction from his noble client. Similarly the orna-mental detail on the stone screen is not that of its period, and is scarcely distinguishable from genuine early 17th-century detail in the now filled arcade on the south side of the south wing.

Notable amongst the objects of art in the hall is a large 15th-century carving in pearwood of a scene from the life of a saint, probably of

South German origin. The furniture includes two sets of chairs dating from the last years of the 17th century. Both sets have elaborately carved cresting and stretchers and turned side rails, the one set being upholstered with red velvet, the other having caned seats and backs. A French 16th-century cabinet, carved with fluted columns, lions' masks, and allegorical female figures, stands against the west wall of the hall, while on the east wall of the stair well there hangs a vellum patent dated at Greenwich, May 1634, and probably the work of Edward Norgate. It is a grant of an augmentation of arms by Charles I to the Earl of Stirling and is decorated with the landing on the coast of Nova Scotia and various hunting and hawking scenes there. A curious feature of the hall is a miniature copy in plaster of the cele-brated classical marble group of the Farnese Bull from the Naples Museum. This rests on a richly carved marble plinth copied from one formerly in the Medici collection, and was acquired for Audley End at the sale of Robert Adam's effects in 1818. The silk heraldic banners, now much tattered, hanging in the hall are emblazoned with bearings of the different families who have owned Audley End. The three guidons and three standards embroidered in silver and crimson on a blue ground (now faded to white) which hang below are those of the first troop of Horse Grenadier Guards of which Sir John Griffin Griffin was Captain and later Colonel between 1766 and 1797.

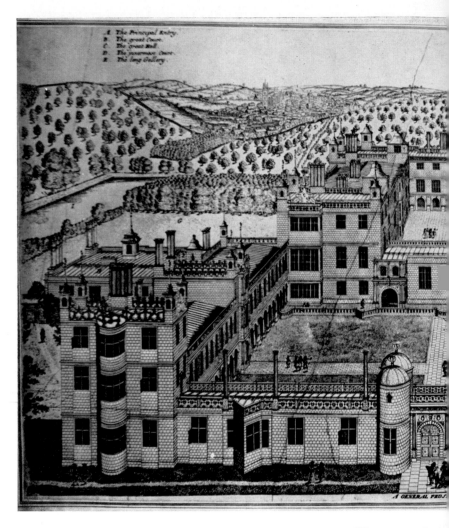

A. The Principal Entry.
B. The great Court.
C. The great Hall.
D. The innermost Court.
E. The long Gallery.

A GENERAL PROS.

WINSTANLEY'S VI

This view, made while the mansion was a Royal I
Hampton Court in size and splendour. In the foreg
its side-wings, enclosing the Base Court, which was
be seen the still surviving Great Hall with its flank
side was remo

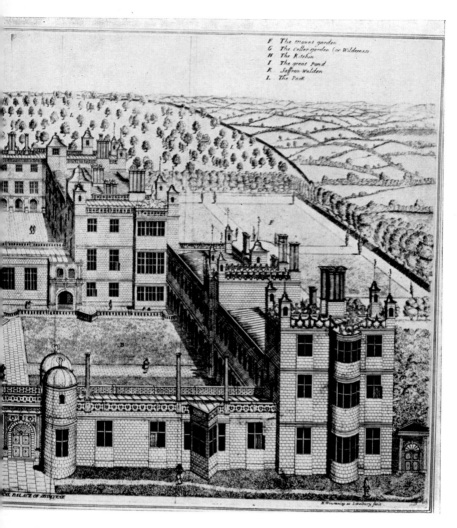

F The mount garden
G The Celler garden (or Wilderness)
H The Kitchin
I The great Pond
K Saffron Walden
L The Park

UDLEY END IN 1676

ows almost the full extent of the buildings, rivalling
the entrance courtyard with the Great Gatehouse and
ay in 1721. On the further side of the courtyard may
es and, beyond, a second courtyard of which th further
dy Portsmouth

Series of paintings of previous owners, commissioned by Lord Braybrooke in 1785.
Left: Margaret, daughter of the first Lord Audley (died 1563); middle: her
husband, Thomas Howard, fourth Duke of Norfolk (1536–72); right: Theophilus,
second Earl of Suffolk (1584–1640)

The row of six Cornwallis and Townshend portraits on the east wall came from Brome Hall in Suffolk at the death of the second Marquess Cornwallis in 1823. Jane, Lady Braybrooke, eldest of his five daughters, inherited a share of the Cornwallis property including the pictures here, the bust of the first Marquess by Bacon in the drawing room, his portrait in the dining room, and the family portraits in the picture gallery. The Howards are represented by Lord Audley's daughter Margaret, Duchess of Norfolk, by Hans Eworth, her husband the fourth Duke, and their grand-daughter the infamous Frances Howard, Countess of Essex and Somerset, whose trial and conviction for the murder of Sir Thomas Overbury was a *cause célèbre* of the 17th century. The Nevilles of Billingbear are shown by portraits of Sir Henry Neville the ambassador, his wife Anne Killigrew, and their son Henry, there is also the whole-length of Edward VI which was seen at Billingbear by George Vertue in 1750. The royal tenure of Audley End is commemorated by the portraits of Charles II on the staircase, and William and Mary, who have two small Lely school portraits in the hall; there is also one of William after Kneller on the staircase and one of Mary by Jan van der Vaart in the dining room.

Left: Edward, first Lord Griffin (died 1710); middle: James, second Lord Griffin (1667–1715); right: Elizabeth, Countess of Portsmouth (1691 1762)

STAIRCASE

On the staircase hangs a small but interesting portrait of Lord Sandwich who was killed at the Battle of Solebay in 1672. It was painted by de Critz for Samuel Pepys and is mentioned in Pepys's Diary for 22 October 1660. The original is by Lely and belongs to Lord Sandwich. The large whole-length of a Cavalier is of Colonel Sir Thomas Lunsford, who married Catherine, daughter of Sir Henry Neville.

SALOON

Before the erection of the stone stair from the hall, this fine room must have been entered either from a stair close to its eastern side or from a room to the north which was destroyed when the stone stair was made. A painted inscription in the northernmost panel of the west wall, whilst epitomising the history of the families from time to time dwelling in the house, states that, apart from the ceiling, the room was refitted by Sir John Griffin Griffin, later Lord Howard de Walden and first Lord Braybrooke. The date of completion of this work, 1785, appears over the north door and his coat of arms and the impaled coats of his two wives are painted on the frieze of the chimney-piece. The decoration and the general appearance of the room may be attributed to this time, but the ceiling and chimney-piece belong to the original early 17th-century house. The latter is a very elaborate example of its kind, but none of the paint is original, nor is the marble fireplace surround. The ceiling, like that of the hall, is divided into compartments, but here the divisions are marked by pendants and strapwork, and the decorative figures consist of ships, mermaids, whales, sea-birds, and fabulous sea-monsters. It is a most interesting collection, which makes the ceiling one of the most notable of its kind and caused the saloon to be known generally as the Fish Room. The frieze of quatrefoils enclosing masks, which runs round the walls between cornice and ceiling, was executed by Joseph Rose, probably Robert Adam's best-known plasterer, in 1763–64. All the panelling dates from the same period. It will be noticed that, in spite of the general appearance of classical design, the clustered capitals at the level of the heads of the painted figures are distinctly gothic in shape. The paintings themselves, by various artists including Biagio Rebecca and Enoch Seeman, represent the predecessors in title to Sir John Griffin Griffin, who appears in the central panel of the west wall. The series was placed in position, as he says in his inscription, 'to commemorate those through whom with gratitude he holds these possessions'. Some came from Dingley Hall in Northamptonshire, then the family seat of the Griffins. The Rebeccas were commissioned by Sir John originally for the breakfast room in his London house and, except for his own portrait (14), were copied from appropriate originals. The portraits of the Duke and Duchess of Norfolk actually bear no resemblance to the persons concerned, being pirated from a picture at Sherborne Castle, *The Visit of Queen Elizabeth to Blackfriars in 1600*. The family scrapbook contains a series by Rebecca of detailed water-colour drawings for these portraits. Among the Braybrooke papers in the Essex Record Office is Rebecca's receipt dated 2 February 1774, 'to six full lengths finished for Breakfast Room at £16 16 0 each'.

Furniture in the saloon includes a set of tapestry-covered chairs and sofas worked with the Howard lion badge and coronet, a large Ottoman and a small French Boulle writing table inlaid with silver and bronze.

DRAWING ROOM

This is a creation of the second or third Lord Braybrooke, and had recently been completed when the latter published his account of

Boulle clock signed 'Balthazar'

Audley End in 1836. It was an enlargement of an existing room which had a fireplace in a different position. The chimney-piece appears to be of the early 17th century, but, if so, it must have been moved from elsewhere when the alteration was made, and painted in conformity with the new style of decoration. The plaster cornice and ceiling were new in 1836, but their general style is that of the early 17th century, and illustrates once more the family's care to ensure that all new work should be in harmony with the old.

At each end of the drawing room is a large Boulle display case in which examples of English and Continental porcelain are exhibited. On the case at the west end of the room stands a bust of Lord Cornwallis by Bacon. The room contains several other pieces of French furniture, notably a small Louis XV table and a Boulle bracket clock of the type known as *religieuse* which has a movement signed by Balthazar, one of a long dynasty of Parisian clockmakers. In the centre of the room is a Chinese Chippendale tea-table of mahogany, the top surrounded by a pierced gallery and resting on legs of cluster column form. The Chinese taste reappears in six armchairs, the backs and arms of which are of 'Chinese railing' lattice work.

The paintings here are mostly 17th-century Dutch and Flemish cabinet pictures, probably collected by Sir John Griffin Griffin. Some of them are of high quality, especially the square Canaletto of Venice (28) on the east wall.

SOUTH LIBRARY

This room also dates from *c.* 1825–30. The cornice and ceiling are similar to those of the drawing room, but the chimney-piece is of earlier date, *c.* 1765–80; a design for it probably by Robert Adam exists in the scrapbook. It is the sole reminder in the room of the time when it was a bedroom, *i.e.* before the early 19th-century alterations, which changed the uses of the rooms on the ground and first floors of this wing. The bookcases were made at the time of these alterations, and there will be seen on the shelves many of the books, in distinctive binding, red and gold chequers, which were the property of Sir John Griffin Griffin, Lord Braybrooke. Books in this binding are shown in a drawing of the old library, which was on the ground floor. The drawing, probably by Robert Adam, *c.* 1765, shows shelves filled with such books. No doubt it was a design for a complete library, with the books all alike in a special binding; but with the extension of the library, when it was removed to the first floor and rearranged in categories, the distinctive books were dispersed. They may be seen, here and there, singly and in groups, both in this room and in the main library. The portrait over the fireplace of Sir John Griffin Griffin, seated in his tent in general's uniform, came likewise from the Adam library where it occupied the place of honour over the fireplace and was set in an architectural frame. His first and second wives in the guise of sibyls, poet and musician, are over the two doors, as they were previously over the doors of the Adam library, and, like the general, were painted by Benjamin West in about 1771. The principal piece of furniture in the room is a large writing table of Louis XV style.

LIBRARY

This sumptuous room was made between 1820 and 1825 by throwing two rooms into one and lowering the floor, which had been 4 ft above that of the adjacent room. The chimney-piece is of early 17th century, but it is known that it was brought from a room in the north wing when the library was made. It was then painted in white and gold, to match the rest of the decoration of the room. The arms are those of the third Lord Braybrooke. The decoration closely resembles that of 1785 in the saloon, since in both places pains have been taken to imitate an older fashion; but they are not identical, as a careful comparison of the lions' heads on the pilasters in the two rooms will show. The plaster ceiling and cornice have features which are repeated in several of the adjacent rooms, showing that most of them were part of one scheme of alteration. The books are a fine collection of classical, foreign, and English books, mainly of the 18th century, but with additions of later volumes on archaeology and ornithology—the especial delight of the third and fourth Lords Braybrooke. The books formerly in the old library on the ground floor may be identified by their distinctive scarlet and gold chequered binding.

This room contains two noteworthy pieces of French furniture. The finer is a Louis XVI writing table stamped by the *ébéniste* P. C. Montigny (1734–1800), but perhaps the more interesting is a small carved wooden armchair of the form known as *caquetoire*. It is of French 16th-century workmanship with later restoration, and was at one time in the possession of the poet Alexander Pope, who gave it to his nurse in his last illness. Later acquired by the Rev. Thomas Ashby, this chair was presented to Lord Braybrooke in 1844. Also worth noting is a writing table of Regency design in Coromandel wood with X-shaped supports. Near the bookcases is an armchair of early 19th-century date, which opens to form a set of library steps. Standing on a small bookcase in the bay is Chantrey's sketch model for a statue of Sir Charles Forbes.

DINING ROOM

Like the library, this room was formed out of two smaller rooms during the alterations of 1820–25. The original dividing wall still partly exists and may be seen. The chimney-pieces are of early 17th-century type, and at first sight seem to be genuine, apart from the gold and white paint and the Royal Arms. They are, however, to all intents and purposes identical in decoration, and such an occurrence would be most unlikely in the 17th century. One at least of them must be a copy. The arms on them are of the kings who owned Audley End in the late 17th century. The plaster ceiling of the western part of this room is like that of the adjacent library, but that of the eastern part is of a somewhat different type. Possibly it is of earlier date, because the room was formerly an important bedroom, which may well have had such an embellishment.

The massive mahogany sideboards no doubt date from the period

Aerial view from north-west

when this room was designed, and the dining table, though of a rather earlier style, may have been made at the same time. Dining chairs, mostly of Chippendale design, are mainly set around the table.

Perhaps the best portraits in the house are in this room, which is dominated by Pine's portrait of King George II (1) and Beechey's Marquess Cornwallis (9). Among the others are Sir Charles Lucas by Dobson (3), the Earl of Pembroke (5) (formerly thought to have been James I's favourite, the Earl of Somerset), a magnificent double portrait by Lely of himself and Hugh May (8), and an interesting small portrait of Mary II by Jan van der Vaart (15).

STAIRCASES AND UPPER (OR PICTURE) GALLERY

The staircases both belong to the original house of the early 17th century. It is not certain that they are in their original positions, and it is probable that the lowest flight of the southern stair has been altered or renewed, but they still represent good, if not the grandest, work of its kind and period.

The Great Drawing Room

The Saloon

The Alcove Room

The Neville Room, with State bed

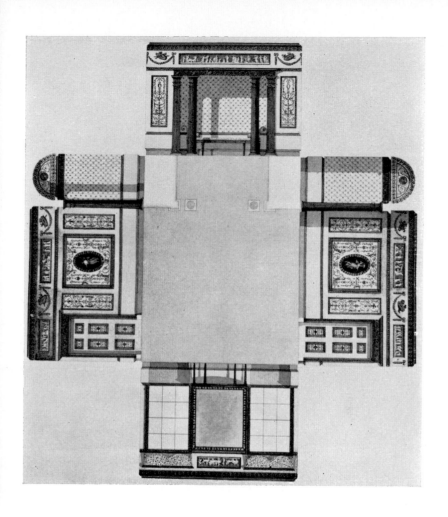

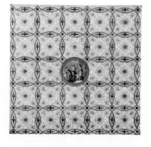

Designs by Robert Adam. Above: for the Alcove Room; right: for its ceiling. The execution of these designs may be seen on the opposite page

The upper gallery between them in its present form is not old. It was built over an open arcade shortly before 1765. The arcade was filled in as it is at present about a hundred years later, and it is probable that the decoration of the gallery, including the chimney-piece in the manner of the early 17th century, dates from this time. This gallery now contains the fine collection of stuffed birds, previously kept in the lower gallery.

On the landing outside the picture gallery is a good series by Lely of Lord Grey of Werke's family. Catherine Grey (2) married Richard Neville of Billingbear and is the ancestress of the Barons Braybrooke.

The picture gallery contains the fine group of Cornwallis portraits brought here by Jane Cornwallis in 1819 on her marriage to the third Lord Braybrooke. The best amongst them are the striking 16th-century portrait of Sir Thomas Cornwallis, attributed to Queen Elizabeth I's sergeant-painter, George Gower (3), and the Restoration painting of the second Lord Cornwallis by J. M. Wright (5).

On the north landing are two Reynolds portraits, of the Earl of Portsmouth (2), whose wife, Elizabeth, successfully claimed a share of the Audley End estate after the death of the tenth Earl of Suffolk, and of Admiral Matthew Whitwell, Sir John Griffin Griffin's brother (1). They are both in fine contemporary carved rococo frames.

NEVILLE ROOM

This is one of a suite of rooms occupying the south side of the north wing: the north-side being occupied by the Howard Rooms. It retains its Jacobean chimney-piece although the fireplace was inserted early in the 18th century. The ceiling is again almost certainly of the 19th century. On the restoration of the Adam drawing room in 1962, the state bed was moved here where the height of the room is in proportion with it. This handsome canopied bed, of late 18th-century date, is hung with its original silk, once blue but now faded, and is richly embroidered with floral patterns on the valances.

The portrait of Queen Charlotte with a small dog is a copy by William Honeyman of Gainsborough's painting at Windsor Castle, 1791. Honeyman's bill for thirty guineas for this and the companion portrait of George III on the hall staircase is in the Braybrooke archives.

CHAPEL

The chapel is a notable example of late 18th-century gothic architecture, completed by 1786, with fittings to match, such as the set of unusual Chippendale chairs in the lobby in the gothic taste, painted cream, and emblazoned with the Griffin arms. This romantic interpretation of gothic architecture is often known as 'Strawberry Hill' Gothic from the house of that name which Horace Walpole, who popularised the style, built between 1749 and 1766. An unpainted olivewood lectern, of the same date as the chairs, stands in the body of the chapel, and Charles Rossi's original model for the tomb of Lord Cornwallis in St. Paul's Cathedral, which was presented to Lord Braybrooke by Lady Mary Singleton, is set against the east wall. The windows were, both of them, interesting examples of English 18th-century painted glass, the work of the well-known York glass painter W. Peckett, and were designed by Biagio Rebecca. Paintings of both still exist, and the fragments of the north window, recently found in the stables, have been pieced together. In 1962 this window was replaced in a replica of its gothic frame. Although dated 1771, it may have been put up somewhat later, and Peckett's bill is dated 1797. The linoleum on the floor is new, but it closely resembles in design and appearance the original floor covering of kamptulicon or oiled cloth, of which portions remain underneath. The chapel has recently (1971) been re-decorated in its original colours, traces of which were found beneath the later paint.

LOWER GALLERY

Until recently this gallery like the one above was filled by the notable collection of stuffed birds formed by the fourth Lord Braybrooke; but these have been moved upstairs into the upper gallery, and also into two rooms on the north side of the south wing where they can be seen to better advantage. This gallery, which forms the connecting link between the wings of the house, contains several fine pieces of furniture, including a pair of English chests of drawers in mahogany, richly mounted with gilt bronze in the style of Louis XV, dating from about 1750.

On the west wall is an interesting collection of views of Audley End and Saffron Walden in about 1790, mostly by William Tomkins. A magnificent Van Goyen, *A River Scene with a Ferry Boat* and two descriptive views of *Montem Day at Eton* by William Evans, are at the foot of the staircase, where a Georgian dolls' house is also exhibited.

THE ADAM ROOMS

When Sir John Griffin Griffin inherited Audley End in 1762, he set himself to complete the alterations begun by his aunt, Lady Portsmouth,

*Part of the ceiling of
the Saloon, showing
panels with various
sea-monsters*

and to embellish it in a fitting manner. At that time he seems not to
have been fully persuaded of the desirability of having decoration in
harmony with the old parts of the house. Robert Adam, rapidly
becoming the most fashionable architect of the day, was therefore
engaged by Sir John not only in the house but also in the gardens.
Internally, apart from extensive repairs including plasterwork, for
example to the ceiling over the Vanbrugh staircase, and the provision
of new fire places, Adam was commissioned to redecorate, and to some
extent remodel, the suite of rooms on the ground floor of the south
wing.

The open colonnade which formed the south side of the south wing
of the 17th-century house had already been filled in *c.* 1740, probably
during the time of the tenth and last Earl of Suffolk. Remains of the
decoration of the additional rooms thus provided have been found in
the form of blue painted wallpaper. The Adam redecoration took in
six rooms, an ante-room, and a vestibule: these were the dining parlour
approached through the now tapestry-hung ante-room at the south
end of the hall; the great drawing room entered through the vestibule
from the east side of the dining parlour; the painted drawing room;
the library occupying the full width of the wing; and then, returning
along the courtyard (north) side of the wing, the withdrawing room
and supper room. Of these the last three no longer remain. The main
works seems to have been completed during 1762–65, but painted
decoration and furnishing continued for some time.

DRESSING ROOM AND BEDROOM

There is little furniture of importance in either of these rooms, though visitors may find the circular pedestal table interesting because of the unusual variety of woods used in the parquetry of the top. The William and Mary chest between the windows is veneered with walnut in an 'oyster' pattern, but has suffered grievously from long exposure to the sun. In the bedroom is a large canopied bed of mahogany, its canopy and hangings of red damask. This bedroom alone of the principal rooms altered early in the 19th century was allowed to be contemporary and retains its agreeable late Georgian marble chimney-piece.

PAINTED DRAWING ROOM

This is the last of the three Adam rooms to survive the early 19th-century alterations. It is also perhaps the most striking, its walls, doors, and ceiling being decorated and painted in the antique manner. A receipt signed by Biagio Rebecca and dated 28 September 1769 for painting in the sitting room survives among the accounts for this work. While Rebecca executed most of the painting, the friezes round the room are after Cipriani. Detailed drawings for the work in this room as for the other Adam rooms are to be found in the scrapbook in the library.

The recess which gives to this room the alternative name of alcove room has a richly painted half-round ceiling and walls hung with silk of striped and floral design. The gilt day-bed with scrolled ends in the alcove and the stools are upholstered in the same material, which is also used for the original window-curtains. Besides the original pier glass between the windows, the room contains a semi-circular side-table of mahogany and gilded gesso, into the front of which is set a panel painted in the style usually associated with Angelica Kauffman, but in this instance probably the work of Biagio Rebecca; and a somewhat similar but smaller side-table of Adam design.

GREAT DRAWING ROOM

This room, one of the finest in the house, has an ornate plaster ceiling by Adam of which the destroyed west end has recently been made good and the whole repainted. The marble chimney-piece is the only Adam one in the house to survive in the original position, but the contemporary carpet probably came from one of the smaller rooms. The suite of furniture was designed by Adam for this room and includes stools, chairs, and sofas with green and gold frames and covered with the same silk as is hung on the walls. Also belonging to this sumptuous set are the two side-tables with tops elaborately veneered in the French taste. These were probably the work of Langlois, a French *ébéniste* working in London between 1760 and 1780, who executed a similar pair for Syon House to Robert Adam's designs about 1763.

The portrait by Zoffany over the fireplace is of Richard Neville Neville, who succeeded to the Billingbear property after the death of the Countess of Portsmouth in 1762. The account 'to Zoffany for my picture—£6' is in the Braybrooke archives. Next to it is a *View of Naples* by Vanvitelli, 1703, with a Genoese merchant ship being careened in the harbour.

Lying between the great drawing room and the dining parlour is a vestibule which originally afforded access from the centre of the house and the Adam rooms to the garden, but the garden-door was replaced by a window in the 19th century. At the same time the vestibule was enlarged for use as a dressing room by taking into it a part of the great drawing room with the consequent destruction of some of the latter's elaborate plaster ceiling. When in 1962 the great drawing room was restored to its original form, the vestibule returned to its proper size. The walls of both were rehung with silk specially woven to the same colours and pattern as the original Spitalfields silk which had both decayed and faded.

Of the pictures in the vestibule, one, the portrait with a sunflower, is a copy, perhaps by Stone, of Van Dyck's self-portrait of 1633–34 in the Duke of Westminster's collection. The sunflower was considered an emblem of royal favour.

THE DINING PARLOUR

The dining parlour occupies the south-west corner of the house and was originally orientated east-west, but Adam placed screens near the north and south ends of the room and formed a vista beyond the south bay window. This necessitated altering the window, which was done on 13 May 1765. Next, the mason's account for 13 June has an item "to unpacking the vause and fixing ditto and clearing away in (the) Mount Garden"—this being the vase that terminates the vista.

As completed by Adam, the room was restrained in its decoration as compared to those which followed. Green and silver-grey paint was used and a frieze with pelta enrichment was limited to the beams across windows and screens.

Unfortunately the dining parlour was extensively shorn of its Adam features in the 19th century when it became the billiard room. The chimney-piece and doorcases were lost and the screens were moved. The opportunity to restore the room to its original appearance was taken in 1962 when extensive repair work became necessary. Missing detail was derived from the Adam drawings in the scrapbook. The doorcases and chimney-piece are carved wood replicas; the screens are original, now in their proper positions; and the tables and pedestals are part of the original furnishing. The dining table is later.

The dining parlour contains the Hans Eworth portrait of the Duchess of Norfolk, signed and dated 1562, one of the most important pictures in the house.

THE GARDENS

Sir John Griffin Griffin's work at Audley End extended beyond the complete restoration of the house, which has already been described, to the replanning of the gardens. These still remain largely the creation of his time.

In April 1763 Lancelot Brown was employed to landscape the grounds in front of the house: reshaping the river, building a ha-ha to the London road, easing the slopes and planting trees—some of the clumps so beloved by Brown may be seen on the hillside west of the house. The river-works were to be terminated at the southern end by a new bridge on the Walden road to be designed by Robert Adam. This scheme not only provided a setting for the house conformable to 18th-century taste but effected practical improvements for the villagers at Audley End by keeping the floods away from the village and providing an adequate bridge for traffic to Saffron Walden.

Elsewhere in the grounds, as on many other contemporary estates, 'Capability' Brown's improvements were garnished with elegant garden buildings, designed here at Audley End by Robert Adam. They included two temples, a Palladian bridge, an obelisk and the rebuilt Lion

Gateway, as well as some garden ornaments. As with the house, works in the gardens were more or less continuous from 1763 until the death of the first Lord Braybrooke in 1797.

First to be built was the *Adam Bridge*—'the intended bridge on the Walden road', already mentioned. In 1763–64, over £500 was spent on masons' work and it must have been completed fairly quickly. Originally it seems to have had a Jacobean-style balustrade, judging both from the accounts and from an architectural drawing of it as it stood in 1781. The present classical balustrade may date from shortly after this. Neither of these periods, however, tallies with the date 1771 carved on one of the roundels set in the spandrels of the arches.

The *Ionic Temple* built in 1770–72 is known as Ring Hill Temple, from the Iron Age hill fort within whose ramparts it is set. It lies to the west of the house beyond the river and the Cambridge road. Built to commemorate the ending of the Seven Years War by the Treaty of Paris of 1763, the temple is circular in plan and contains a single room with an enriched plaster dome. The painted stools which Adam designed to fit this room have been restored, but are displayed in the house for their protection.

North-west of the house, the *Elysian Garden* consists of a tree-lined glade bisected by the river Cam which enters from the south via a

Opposite:
Temple of Concord

Right:
Ring Hill Temple

rustic cascade and disappears northwards beneath the *Palladian Bridge* which terminates the vista. Robert Adam provided several earlier designs, more imposing but perhaps less charming than this small tetrastyle Ionic bridge temple which is now known as the Tea House Bridge and dates from 1783.

North-east and east of the house are two commemorative structures. The first, a tall *Column* bearing an inscription to the memory of the Lady Portsmouth and surmounted by a typical classical urn, acknowledges Sir John's debt of gratitude to his benefactress. Adam provided a design for a column in 1763 but its execution was delayed until 1774–76. It occupies a commanding position and can be reached by a footpath. King George III's recovery from his first attack of insanity is commemorated in an inscription on the monumental Corinthian temple known as the *Temple of Concord*, which is set on the rising ground east of the house. This seems to have been the last major garden building erected and dates from 1790–91.

Apart from the garden buildings as such, the Lion Gate with its Coade stone lion and flanking vases also dates from this period. Its re-

The Tea House Bridge from the south-west

building was probably necessitated by the improvements to the Walden road.

Though the layout of the grounds is that of the 18th century, the 19th century saw much planting and the provision of lodges, the boathouse and the rose garden with its otter pit.

Despite all changes the original early 17th-century stables remain as the most striking building in the grounds. The interior, however, is closed to visitors while it is being adapted to house a collection of agricultural implements, which has been collected by the Saffron Walden Museum.

Printed in England for Her Majesty's Stationery Office by Wells KPL
Swindon Press, Swindon, Wilts.

Dd. 504667 K483 1/74 Gp 469